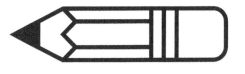

THIS
LEARN-TO-DRAW BOOK
BELONGS TO:

_____

_____

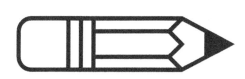

HOW TO USE THIS BOOK:

1. **FOLLOW THE STEPS ON THE LEFT PAGE.**

2. **PRACTICE YOUR DRAWING ON THE RIGHT PAGE.**

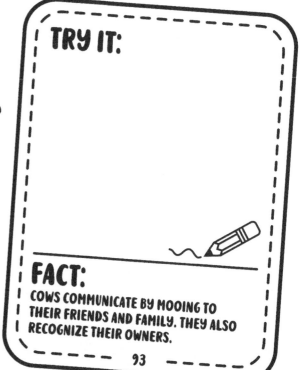

3. **COLOR THE ANIMAL WHEN YOU'RE DONE.**

4. **LEARN INTERESTING FACTS ABOUT THE ANIMAL.**

LET'S LEARN TO DRAW ANIMALS:

BEAR
PAGES 8-9

CAT
PAGES 10-11

DOG
PAGES 12-13

ELEPHANT
PAGES 14-15

FROG
PAGES 16-17

GIRAFFE
PAGES 18-19

PENGUIN
PAGES 20-21

BUTTERFLY
PAGES 22-23

RABBIT
PAGES 24-25

LION
PAGES 26-27

LET'S LEARN TO DRAW ANIMALS:

MOUSE
PAGES 28-29

MONKEY
PAGES 30-31

OWL
PAGES 32-33

SLOTH
PAGES 34-35

PIG
PAGES 36-37

PANDA
PAGES 38-39

LADYBUG
PAGES 40-41

TURTLE
PAGES 42-43

HORSE
PAGES 44-45

WOLF
PAGES 46-47

LET'S LEARN TO DRAW ANIMALS:

BEE
PAGES 48-49

DEER
PAGES 50-51

RACCOON
PAGES 52-53

OCTOPUS
PAGES 54-55

ZEBRA
PAGES 56-57

SNAIL
PAGES 58-59

BEAVER
PAGES 60-61

FOX
PAGES 62-63

BISON
PAGES 64-65

OTTER
PAGES 66-67

LET'S LEARN TO DRAW ANIMALS:

BAT
PAGES 68-69

MOLE
PAGES 70-71

DUCK
PAGES 72-73

JELLYFISH
PAGES 74-75

SQUIRREL
PAGES 76-77

TURKEY
PAGES 78-79

CRAB
PAGES 80-81

SNAKE
PAGES 82-83

DRAGONFLY
PAGES 84-85

AXOLOTL
PAGES 86-87

LET'S LEARN TO DRAW ANIMALS:

SEAL
PAGES 88-89

CHICKEN
PAGES 90-91

COW
PAGES 92-93

HEDGEHOG
PAGES 94-95

SHEEP
PAGES 96-97

KOALA
PAGES 98-99

TIGER
PAGES 100-101

CROCODILE
PAGES 102-103

HIGHLAND COW
PAGES 104-105

CAPYBARA
PAGES 106-107

BEAR

TRY IT:

FACT:
BEARS LOVE HONEY, BUT THEY ALSO EAT FISH, BERRIES, AND PLANTS.

CAT

TRY IT:

FACT:
CATS CAN JUMP UP TO SIX TIMES THEIR BODY LENGTH IN ONE LEAP.

DOG

12

TRY IT:

FACT:
DOG'S NOSE PRINT IS AS UNIQUE AS A HUMAN'S FINGERPRINT. NO TWO ARE THE SAME.

ELEPHANT

TRY IT:

FACT:
ELEPHANTS CAN USE THEIR TRUNKS TO PICK UP TINY OBJECTS AND EVEN DRINK WATER.

FROG

16

TRY IT:

FACT:
FROGS DON'T DRINK WATER.
THEY ABSORB IT THROUGH THEIR SKIN.

GIRAFFE

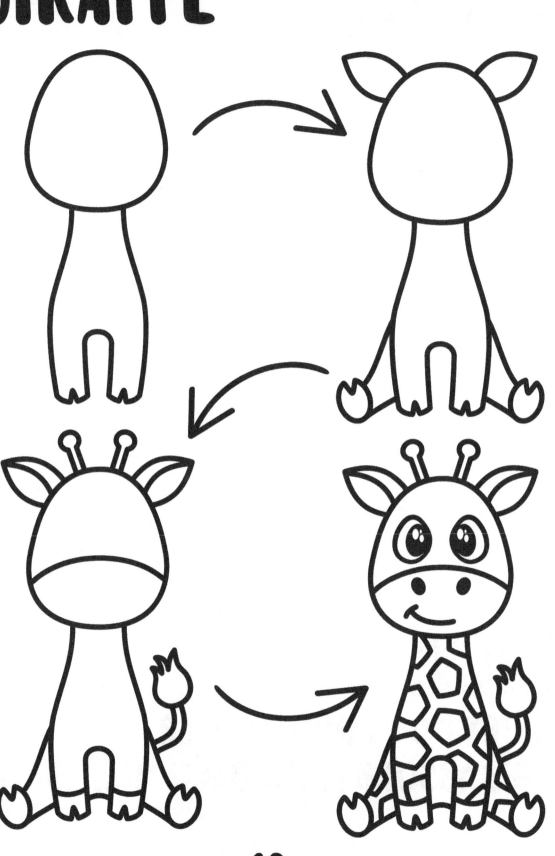

TRY IT:

FACT:
GIRAFFES ARE THE TALLEST LAND ANIMALS. EACH GIRAFFE'S COAT PATTERN IS UNIQUE, JUST LIKE A FINGERPRINT.

PENGUIN

20

TRY IT:

FACT:
PENGUINS CAN'T FLY, BUT THEY ARE AMAZING SWIMMERS.

BUTTERFLY

22

TRY IT:

FACT:
BUTTERFLIES TASTE WITH THEIR FEET AND CAN SEE COLORS THAT HUMANS CAN'T.

RABBIT

24

TRY IT:

FACT:
RABBITS' TEETH NEVER STOP GROWING, SO THEY NEED TO CHEW A LOT.

TRY IT:

FACT:
A LION'S ROAR CAN BE HEARD FROM 8 KILOMETERS AWAY.

MOUSE

28

TRY IT:

FACT:
MICE CAN SQUEEZE THROUGH TINY HOLES AS SMALL AS A PENCIL.

MONKEY

30

TRY IT:

FACT:
MONKEYS USE MANY DIFFERENT SOUNDS TO COMMUNICATE.

OWL

32

TRY IT:

FACT:
OWLS CAN TURN THEIR HEADS ALMOST ALL THE WAY AROUND.

SLOTH

34

TRY IT:

FACT:
SLOTHS ARE SO SLOW THAT ALGAE GROW ON THEIR FUR.

PIG

36

TRY IT:

FACT:
PIGS ARE VERY INTELLIGENT AND CAN LEARN TRICKS.

PANDA

38

TRY IT:

FACT:
PANDAS EAT BAMBOO ALMOST ALL DAY LONG - UP TO 14 HOURS A DAY.

LADYBUG

TRY IT:

FACT:
LADYBUGS ARE CONSIDERED A SYMBOL OF GOOD LUCK IN MANY CULTURES.

TURTLE

42

TRY IT:

FACT:
SOME TURTLES CAN LIVE FOR MORE THAN 100 YEARS.

HORSE

44

TRY IT:

FACT:
HORSES CAN SLEEP BOTH LYING DOWN AND STANDING UP.

TRY IT:

FACT:
WOLVES COMMUNICATE BY HOWLING TO FIND THEIR PACK MEMBERS.

BEE

TRY IT:

FACT:
BEES DANCE TO TELL OTHER BEES WHERE TO FIND FOOD.

DEER

50

TRY IT:

FACT:
A DEER'S ANTLERS FALL OFF EVERY YEAR AND GROW BACK.

RACCOON

52

TRY IT:

FACT:
RACCOONS ARE VERY CURIOUS. THEY LOVE TO EXPLORE AND DISCOVER NEW THINGS.

OCTOPUS

54

TRY IT:

FACT:
AN OCTOPUS CAN CHANGE COLOR TO BLEND IN WITH ITS SURROUNDINGS.

ZEBRA

TRY IT:

FACT:
NO TWO ZEBRAS HAVE THE SAME STRIPE PATTERN. THEY ARE ALL UNIQUE.

SNAIL

TRY IT:

FACT:
SNAILS CAN SLEEP FOR UP TO THREE YEARS.

BEAVER

TRY IT:

FACT:
BEAVERS' TEETH NEVER STOP GROWING, SO THEY CHEW WOOD TO KEEP THEM SHORT.

FOX

62

TRY IT:

FACT:
FOXES SLEEP DURING THE DAY.
THEY ARE MOSTLY ACTIVE AT NIGHT.

BISON

TRY IT:

FACT:
BISON ARE THE LARGEST LAND ANIMALS IN NORTH AMERICA.

OTTER

66

TRY IT:

FACT:
OTTERS HOLD HANDS WHILE SLEEPING SO THEY DON'T DRIFT APART IN THE WATER.

BAT

68

TRY IT:

FACT:
BATS ARE THE ONLY MAMMALS THAT CAN TRULY FLY.

MOLE

70

TRY IT:

FACT:
MOLES CAN DIG TUNNELS SUPER FAST, SOMETIMES UP TO 5 METERS PER HOUR.

DUCK

72

TRY IT:

FACT:
A DUCK'S FEATHERS ARE WATERPROOF, SO THEY NEVER GET WET.

JELLYFISH

TRY IT:

FACT:
JELLYFISH ARE MOSTLY WATER, MAKING THEM INCREDIBLY SOFT AND TRANSPARENT.

SQUIRREL

TRY IT:

FACT:
SQUIRRELS HELP FORESTS GROW BY OFTEN FORGETTING WHERE THEY BURIED THEIR NUTS.

TURKEY

78

TRY IT:

FACT:
A TURKEY'S GOBBLE CAN BE HEARD FROM A KILOMETER AWAY.

CRAB

80

TRY IT:

FACT:
CRABS WALK SIDEWAYS BECAUSE THEIR LEGS ARE DESIGNED FOR SIDEWAYS MOVEMENT.

SNAKE

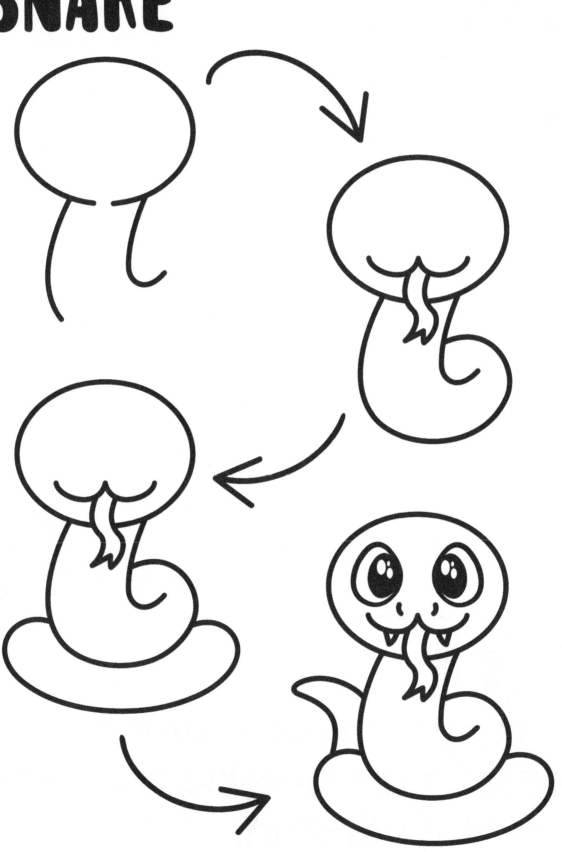

TRY IT:

FACT:
SNAKES SMELL WITH THEIR TONGUES.

DRAGONFLY

TRY IT:

FACT:
DRAGONFLIES HAVE BEEN AROUND SINCE THE TIME OF THE DINOSAURS.

AXOLOTL

TRY IT:

FACT:
AXOLOTLS CAN BREATHE BOTH IN WATER AND ON LAND.

SEAL

88

TRY IT:

FACT:
SEALS CAN HOLD THEIR BREATH FOR UP TO 30 MINUTES UNDERWATER.

CHICKEN

TRY IT:

FACT:
CHICKENS CAN REMEMBER OVER 100 DIFFERENT FACES.

COW

92

TRY IT:

FACT:
COWS COMMUNICATE BY MOOING TO THEIR FRIENDS AND FAMILY. THEY ALSO RECOGNIZE THEIR OWNERS.

HEDGEHOG

94

TRY IT:

FACT:
HEDGEHOGS ARE NOCTURNAL AND MOST ACTIVE AT NIGHT WHILE SEARCHING FOR FOOD.

SHEEP

96

TRY IT:

FACT:
SHEEP HAVE EXCELLENT MEMORY. THEY CAN REMEMBER FACES FOR UP TO TWO YEARS.

KOALA

TRY IT:

FACT:
KOALAS SLEEP UP TO 20 HOURS A DAY.

TIGER

100

TRY IT:

FACT:
TIGER'S STRIPES ARE LIKE A FINGERPRINT. NO TWO ARE THE SAME.

CROCODILE

TRY IT:

FACT:
CROCODILES HAVE BEEN AROUND SINCE THE TIME OF THE DINOSAURS.

HIGHLAND COW

TRY IT:

FACT:
HIGHLAND COWS HAVE LONG, FLUFFY HAIR TO KEEP WARM IN COLD WEATHER.

CAPYBARA

TRY IT:

FACT:
CAPYBARAS ARE THE WORLD'S LARGEST RODENTS AND LOVE TO SWIM.

IMPRESSUM
ARTUR BAUER
ARTURB_BUSINESS@ICLOUD.COM

INDEPENDENTLY PUBLISHED
© 2025 ARTUR BAUER
ALL RIGHTS RESERVED